FAMILY CIRCUS®
I
COULD
HEAR
CHEWING

Bil Keane

FAWCETT GOLD MEDAL • NEW YORK

A Fawcett Gold Medal Book
Published by Ballantine Books
Copyright © 1983, by Cowles Syndicate, Inc.
Copyright © 1987 by King Features Syndicate, Inc.

ISBN 0-449-13372-9

Manufactured in the United States of America

First Edition: April 1988

"I need a jar, Mommy, quick! This guy tickles."

"You go down here to the climbin' tree, over Mrs. Cobb's fence, hang a left at Max's house, through Boyd's back yard, under the hedge. . . ."

"That's a neat shirt, Daddy. Can I have it when you grow out of it?"

"It's OK, Mommy. Only half of
it broke."

"Mommy, can we get one of these plastic balls
with the windows in it?"

"If she won't come out, let's fire tear gas
through her window."

"If I plant this seed will it grow
a hamburger bun?"

"Daddy, will you hitch up the video
games for me?"

"Keep your kite out of our air space."

"It'd be hard to put any 'raffiti on THAT fence."

"Hi, Mom! Billy wants to know if I can eat here."

"Can't you buy instant flower seeds?"

"You sure have a big pocketbook."

"I'm going to be in the school play, Dahling."

"Can I change my shirt, Mommy?
Everybody's read this one."

"You don't hear me practicin' because
I'm doin' it in my head."

"Mommy? The barber won't give me a crewcut
unless I bring a note from you."

"Mommy, what comes after 'elebenteen'?"

"This is where Mommy puts all the stuff that doesn't belong anywhere."

"Why can't I ride MY bike in the house?"

"Smile, Grandma! God's taking our picture!"

"Turtles never get out of low gear."

"What ending is it, Daddy?"

"Who called me 'Mommy Dearest'?"

"It says 'I-O-U a quarter. Love, the Tooth Fairy.' "

"The stuff in the door is lucky. It gets
lots of rides."

"Why does Grandma drink decapitated coffee?"

"All the kids in my class were promoted, but
Miss McElfresh got left back."

"Some cats don't like to ride in
doll carriages."

"There'll be no more clinking of glasses."

"Mommy, will you make this TV behave?"

". . . and it's caffeine-free, too!"

"The wrapping on this chicken doesn't
taste as good as yours."

"You're better than just a father. You're
a DADDY!"

"Daddy's Father's Day present will be all ready as soon as we finish the cage."

"Daddy, why don't you get your company to
close up for the summer like our
school does?"

"Don't be afraid. The lightning won't strike you as long as Mommy's out here."

"Can I have one without freckles?"

"We're rich! Mommy got 200 new checks!"

"My camel feels right at home."

"Daddy hasn't read the paper yet. It's still neat."

"Could you put out fires with that stuff?"

"I'll be back in a moment — following those messages."

"When you put ice cream on it it's
called pie Alamo."

"Don't let go of me, Daddy! Don't let go!"

"Is that lady wearing her WHOLE bathing suit, Mommy?"

"I'm buildin' a pyramid. It's easier."

"They're not 'TATO CHIPS, Jeffy. They're BITATO SHIPS!"

"Terry's lucky. His house is so small that he and his brother have bunk beds."

"Mommy, you didn't really like that lamp Aunt
Nancy gave us, did you?"

"Can I have another roll of corn?"

"Medium . . . medium . . . medium. . . ."
"LARGE please, Daddy."

"I don't think I'll ever get into the major leagues.
I'm not allowed to spit!"

"Mommy, is this grasshopper a boy or a girl?"

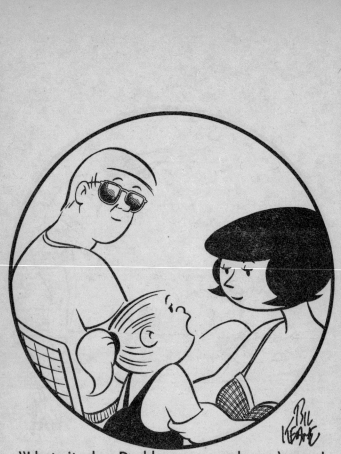

"I hate it when Daddy wears sunglasses 'cause I can't tell when he's winkin'."

"I had my head underwater and now this ear
doesn't listen!"

"Our ball set off the alarm on
Mr. Anderson's car!"

"I'm going ashore."

"Mommy! Look what happens when you mix some
green mouthwash and some red mouthwash —
BROWN mouthwash!"

"These are the baggage tags they put on
Daddy when he was in the Army."

"Oh, good! That's the 'rad' sitter with
the 'totally awesome' boyfriend."

"It's gonna be an island."

"We're takin' Barfy to the V...E...T."

"How's anybody s'posed to read these books
of yours? There are no pictures in 'em!"

"Mommy! Billy's bein' Mr. T!"

"Pandas are just bears painted different."

"Mommy! You didn't wash yesterday's pants,
did you?"

"Couldn't I just LICK my hands clean?"

"Billy said a bad word."

"Why do bridges always have hills on them?"

"Boy! You'd need a lot of rope to hang a
swing from that!"

"Daddy, are you lost or are we going for a ride?"

"Which is this, Daddy — a woods, a forest or
a jungle?"

"I'll take that. It's our first-aid equipment!"

"If anyone gets lost, just follow the first ant you
see and I'm sure he'll bring you back here!"

"I TOOK a bath before we came!"

"How much longer till it gets dark, Mommy?"

"We hafta put the food up there to keep it away
from bears, squirrels, raccoons and Jeffy!"

"Dinner's takin' too long to cook, Mommy. We
should've brought our microwave oven!"

"Time to get up yet, Daddy?"
"Go back to sleep. It's not quite 10 o'clock!"

"It's only an owl. Now, get back in your
own sleeping bag!"

"Barfy's never had so many trees to choose from."

"Once upon a time there lived a ghost who . . . .
Aw, come on! Stop giggling. This is
supposed to be spooky!"

"Stop bouncing on those air mattresses!"

"Daddy's lettin' his whiskers grow. Why can't
I let my dirt grow?"

"My mattress had a flat!"

"PJ's eating his marshmallows raw!"

"I guess tents aren't very good for throwing balls against."

"The weatherman on TV didn't say anything about this, Daddy. Can we sue him?"

". . . or coloring books or board games or
puzzles or storybooks or . . . ."

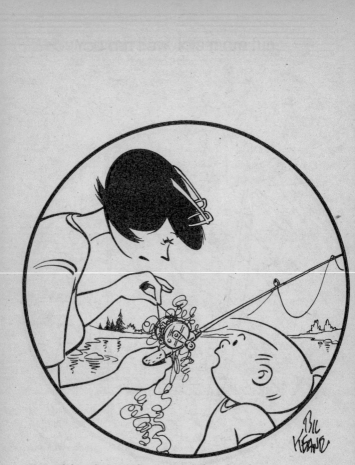

"Daddy always fixes it with a knife. He cuts the whole thing off and starts over."

"Mommy, this is Tommy Libonate from the RV by
the lake. Can he stay overnight?"

"Where can I buy a post card? Grandma said to
be sure to send her one."

"I'm movin' to the non-smoking section."

"When we get home tonight can we all sleep in
the tent out in our back yard?"

"I saw the queen on TV. That sure isn't a good
picture of her on our deck of cards."

"Look, everybody! A straight rainbow!"

"Why does a piano's alphabet only go
up to 'G'?"

"Grandma named this dessert after my
doll — Strawberry Shortcake!"

"But I was just tryin' to find out how much
toothpaste was left."

"Where do ply trees grow?"

"We're havin' Barbie cute ribs!"

"I didn't know banks had WALK-IN windows, too!"

"Which is this, Mommy, a lasso, a lariat, a noose
or a rope?"

"Why don't the numbers move and talk like they do on 'Sesame Street'?"

"Mommy put oinkment on my cut!"

"Hurry up, Daddy! They're having roll call!"

"I can see the handwriting on the wall."

"I didn't do it, Mommy!"

"Uncle Tom's car has a new invention on it — it's called a stick shift!"

"Oooh! This program gives me goof bumps!"

"Not bad, but I'd advise you not to plan on a
career in the military."

"I bit my tongue, Mommy! Will you kiss it?"

"Hang around in case I need some backup!"

"I wish Sam was a cartoon dog — then he could talk!"

"My mom says we're not gonna carry any more
ads on our clothes unless we get paid for it."

"Look! I'm a robic dancer! I'm dancin' in
my robe!"

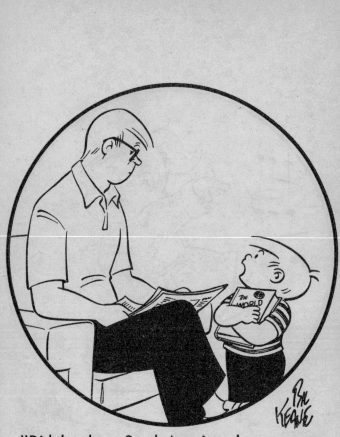

"Did they have South America when you were in school?"

"Look! It's a filled moon tonight!"

"I want to kiss you one more time while I'm
still 5."

"If we promise not to ask for anything will
you buy us something?"

"When will I be old enough to stay up till
prime time?"

"Look how big I am, Mommy! I'm up
to here already!"

You can have lots more fun
with
BIL KEANE and
THE FAMILY CIRCUS